ESFP: Understanding &
Relating with the Performer
MBTI Personality Types Series

By: Clayton Geoffreys

Table of Contents

Foreword

Have you ever been curious about why you behave certain ways? Well I know I have always pondered this question. When I first learned about psychology in high school, I immediately was hooked. Learning about the inner workings of the human mind fascinated me. Human beings are some of the most impressive species to ever walk on this earth. Over the years, one thing I've learned from my life experiences is that having a high degree of self-awareness is critical to get to where you want to go in life and to achieve what you want to accomplish. A person who is not self-aware is a person who lives life blindly, accepting what some label as fate. I began intensely studying psychology to better understand myself, and through my journey, I discovered the Myers Brigg Type Indicator (MBTI), a popular personality test that distinguishes between sixteen types of individuals. I hope to cover some of the most prevalent personality types of the MBTI test and share my findings with you through a series of books. Rather than just reading this for the sake of reading it though, I want you to reflect on the information that will be shared with you. Hopefully from reading *ESFP: Understanding & Relating with the Performer*, I can pass along some of the abundance of information I have learned about ESFPs in general, how they view the world, as well as their greatest strengths and weaknesses. Thank you for purchasing my book. Hope you enjoy and if you do, please do not forget to leave a review! Also, check out my website at claytongeoffreys.com to join my exclusive list where I let you know about my latest books. To thank you for your purchase, you can go to my site to download a free copy of *33 Life Lessons: Success Principles, Career Advice & Habits of Successful People*. In the book, you'll learn from some of the greatest thought leaders of different industries on what it takes to become successful and how to live a great life.

Cheers,

Clayton Geoffrey

An Introduction to MBTI

Susan Cain's book *Quiet: The Power of Introverts in a World That Can't Stop Talking* re-ignited a discussion in society. When placed alongside Extroverts (E), it was made clear to many Introverts (I) (particularly those in the U.S.) that they needed to somehow transform into outgoing and aggressive types in order to be successful in the business world. Cain's book provided real-life examples of prosperous Introverts (I), putting a focus on the Myers-Briggs inventory once again.

The concepts for the inventory came directly from Carl Jung, a prominent psychologist and colleague of Sigmund Freud. Jung was an Introvert (I) himself, who emphasized human behaviors and their commonalities in his work. Katharine Cook Briggs and her daughter Isabel Briggs Myers studied Jung's work extensively and decided to develop an inventory that could put his ideas to practical use. The inventory was originally created to help women entering the workforce to discover which industrial jobs they were most suited for. Today, it is used in career and marriage counseling, marketing, and a variety of other fields.[1]

Jung described three dimensions in his work: Extroversion-Introversion (EI), Sensing-Intuition (SI), and Thinking-Feeling (TF). Myers and Briggs felt that another dimension should be added, one that would show how we react to the outside world. This dimension is the Judging-Perceiving (JP) preference and it is regarded as a major contribution to the Myers-Briggs inventory.[2]

The most current version of the inventory includes 93 questions (88 in the European version) that ask the test-taker to choose one of two possible answers to each question. The scores that are obtained are then used to identify a person's preferences in each of the four dimensions, as well as their strength. The chosen preferences are innate and dominant, but our nondominant functions can also be developed if we choose. After the scores from each dimension are combined, they will form one of sixteen personality types.

The Four Dimensions of the MBTI

Jung's theory implies that you have an ingrained preference for one function or attitude in each of the four categories. The four groups look at how you are energized, the type of information you pay attention to, how you make decisions and your attitude when it comes to the outside world.[3] Keep in mind that each preference is equally valuable and they should not be considered good or bad. Each function will interact with the other three characteristics that make up a type to form a unique personality.

1. Extroversion (E) vs. Introversion (I)[4]

Extroverted types need constant stimulation that you will often find in the outside environment. You rely on social contact for much of your energy and usually have great communication skills that you use effortlessly.

As an Introvert, you favor solitude and privacy, as you

can retreat to a rich and imaginative inner world to replenish your energy. You are thoughtful and contemplative, often preferring to think before you speak.

2. Intuition (N) vs. Sensing (S)[5]

If you have a preference for Intuition (I), it is likely that you are open to possibilities and may perceive information through means that are not "visible to the senses." In certain situations, you may ignore realities in favor of these possibilities.

If your scores indicate that you use Sensing (S), you can interpret this to mean that you gather information through your five senses. You are grounded in reality and your immediate environment.

3. Feeling (F) vs. Thinking (T)[6]

A Feeling (F) type is likely to be concerned with incorporating their values and the opinions of others into their decision-making process. Harmonious environments are important to you and you may use your innate understanding of human nature to ensure such an atmosphere.

Scoring highest in the Thinking (T) category implies that you base your decisions on logic as well as a fair amount of analysis. You can be very objective when needed, especially since you are focused on justice and fairness.

4. Perceiving (P) vs. Judging (J)[7]

For those with a Perceiving (P) attitude, decisions need not be made until all information has been considered. Since new information is constantly made available, many Perceivers (P) are quick to amend their decisions.

Judging (J) types are quite different, in that you prefer for any decisions you make to be final. To this end, you are often very organized and will only consider finite amounts of information when making your choice.

Why is the Myers-Briggs Type Indicator Significant?

The Myers-Briggs inventory is used in many types of settings and its results can be applied to the education, career, and relationship arenas. The inventory is both broad and specific enough to include the general population and its subgroups. It is one of the most widely used personality assessments in the world and has been translated into over 40 languages. It is unique in that it describes our motivations, reactions, and other thought processes, in addition to widely held traits.[8]

Improved communication and a better understanding of oneself and others is the general outcome of an analysis of the test results. Many organizations now see how and why interactions between Introverts (I) and Extroverts (E) or those with Sensing (S) versus Intuitive (I) preferences can be rife with conflict at

11

times. They can also begin to find ways to remedy these situations with solutions that are tailored to each personality. The end result is improved morale and teamwork among employees, leading to greater productivity.

The results can be used similarly in the education arena. Teaching a student with a Thinking (T) preference about theories and their possible directions is likely to bore them, while Intuitive (I) students will be very engrossed in the subject matter. Likewise, too much group work can overwhelm Introverts (I) but provide Extroverts (E) with some much-needed opportunities to engage in social interaction.

When it comes to a person's career, the Myers-Briggs inventory is sure to provide many options for every personality type. Although the two middle letters of your type are most significant in determining the vocation that would be most satisfying for you, it is important to take into account all four letters. For example, if your middle letters are SF (Sensing + Feeling), you may find that you prefer jobs in which you can maintain a great deal of autonomy when it comes to assignments and use your strong people skills. However, if you are an Introvert (I), you will be happiest working with others one-on-one. As an Extrovert, you will prefer being surrounded by others as you complete your work.[9]

The inventory can even be useful when it comes to romantic relationships. Figuring out the secret to long-lasting connections has been a concern of many for quite a while. Although no test can provide a definite answer to this question, careful consideration of certain types can provide insight into relationships that may have a fighting chance. If you identify as a person with a Judging (J) preference, it is more likely that you will prefer organization, stability, and concrete decisions in your life. How then, would it feel to date someone with a strong Perceiving (P) function, who prefers to deal with things as they arise and changes their mind frequently?

When compared to other personality assessments, the Myers-Briggs inventory can provide us with a more thorough explanation of our motivations. The results of the test can be used to improve many areas of our lives in very significant ways.

Uncovering the "Performers": Who is an ESFP?

ESFPs are the 6[10] most common Myers-Briggs type, making up a little over 10% of the population.[10] Your nickname "The Performer" is an apt descriptor, as you love entertaining others and being the center of attention. Extremely sociable and playful, you hate being alone. This is usually not an issue for you, thanks to your charming personality. Most people love being around you, as you always seem to know the latest jokes and stories. Hanging out with you often feels like being at a party 24/7.

When compared to other types, specifically those that share Sensing (S) and Perceiving (P) traits, you share many common qualities yet also differ in several ways.[11] Like other SP types, you are fond of using tools and use sensible and down-to-earth language to communicate with others. You have a passion and talent for using computers, as you seem to know exactly what to use them for. You differ from other SP types in the extreme emphasis that you put on the present. Past and future experiences are of no use to you, which can sometimes lead to hedonism on your part.[12]

As an ESFP, you usually know when and how much to indulge yourself. Still, your impulsive nature and desire to live life to the fullest can lead to you giving in quite easily when it comes to temptation. Your impulsiveness may also rear its head when you are confronted with variety. If an experience turns out negatively or different from what you planned, you take it in stride. Another reaction you may have is to blame others if things do not turn out well.

You are likely to accomplish all of your goals when placed in the right situations, but your tolerance for anxiety is the lowest out of all of the types. It is not surprising then that you hate conflict and will often ignore any unpleasantness that may color a situation until it is no longer possible. You are most comfortable around upbeat people and will usually attempt to change a serious situation into a light-hearted one. Accomplishing this task is not difficult, since you have a knack for lifting others' spirits.[13]

Your Feeling (F) trait gives you the ability to quickly and accurately assess those around you. This quality is part of what makes you such as charming person and it is often the case that you are voted "friendliest" or "best sport" in high school.[14]

When it comes to school, ESFPs are often found in the class clown position. You are not particularly interested in academics, but will adhere to deadlines when asked. However, your teachers may be disappointed in the lack of effort present in your work. In your spare time, you often enjoy playing on sports teams, or participating in school plays or other activities that permit you to fool around with your friends.

After completing your education, you will prefer careers that allow you to work with others in large or small groups. Technical and scientific occupations do not hold your interest for long; still you can excel in positions where you use your talents to sell to others. Your social skills also make you excellent real estate agents, teachers, and social workers. In this last career, you can exercise your innate ability to calm others when they are in crisis.[15]

ESFPs are also more comfortable learning from hands-on experiences and should search for careers that require this. You do not need a plan most of the time, thanks to your ability to adapt. When you run into a roadblock, you have no qualms about going in a different direction. First, though, you will look at the available facts and figures to help you come up with a practical solution.[16]

As parents and mates, you are exciting and unpredictable. This last trait has been known to cause anxiety in your loved ones. You are happiest when your home is filled with people, and you will spend these times mingling and joking with everyone. You make warm and loving friends, but those who get to know you understand that you do not take their relationships seriously.[17]

Your type is open-minded, tolerant, and adaptable, qualities that draw others to you. Your excitement and zest for life can lead you into some sticky situations that may lead you into temptation or have negative consequences. These events do not faze you, as you prefer to stay light-hearted and happy no matter what. These talents make you a much-needed presence in the lives of many.

Why are ESFPs Indispensable Leaders?

If you are looking for someone to be the face of a company, try using an ESFP. Both gregarious and confident, your type knows how to make the best of an opportunity, particularly when all eyes are on you. When combined with your social skills and open-mindedness, you make a wonderful leader for many organizations.

Your type is enthusiastic and willing to cooperate with many different personalities. You accept everyone's quirks without hesitation and work with them accordingly. ESFPs are also one of the few types who can effectively communicate in a variety of situations, whether in person or over the phone. You function best in a harmonious environment and endeavor to make such a setting a reality. This is normally accomplished by showing appreciation for the contributions of your team members, in addition to using your talent for defusing tension in potentially volatile situations.

Often, you will also encourage and guide others to use their talents to the best of their ability.[18]

As a leader, you always attempt to promote teamwork over individual input. You have a knack for facilitating this type of interaction and inspire others with your ability to inject fun into every task. Although you expect to be followed and not questioned, people genuinely enjoy working for you and with you. One reason for this is that you will not ask anyone to complete a task that you are not willing to do yourself. In fact, you are known to work alongside your employees doing just that, as you feel that asserting your authority and social status is secondary to making everyone believe that they add value to the team. Playing favorites is not your style and you will allow everyone to speak their minds without fear of retribution. Unlike many leaders, you often solicit feedback and input from others, and use it to guide the next steps you take.[19]

With an ESFP leader, you can be sure that everyone will know which project components they are responsible for, as these types have the ability to give clear and concise instructions. Realistic in your approach, it is not uncommon for you to reach and surpass given goals by focusing on the present. Although you put your best effort into the initial phase of a project, you also have a concrete idea of the path that it should follow and where it will end up. One of your greatest talents as a leader is your knack for spotting trouble well in advance. When this occurs, you are able to handle it brilliantly, improvising shortcuts and confronting new issues as they come up. On the other hand, if a project is unable to be salvaged, you can accept the outcome and move on quickly.[20]

As an ESFP, you have the ability to work without being given much direction from higher-ups and can easily find the resources needed to complete your duties. When it comes to hectic environments, you can function quite well and may be found handling several assignments at once. You will lead by example and guide those who may feel overwhelmed by such a setting.

Your flexibility and adaptability are among the assets that allow you to thrive in a leadership position. When these are used alongside your talent for working with many personalities, you will surely rise through the ranks quickly. Your sociability makes you a very likable person, which may in turn; give you opportunities to take on a more public role in an organization. The combination of all of these gifts is rare and should be considered the hallmark of a great leader.

The 7 Greatest Strengths of an ESFP

Each Myers-Briggs personality type has talents, which, if used properly, can make a positive impact on the lives of others. As an ESFP, you are unique in that the level of generosity and genuineness present in you make you a person that others are likely to flock to.

1. Bolder and More Assertive than Most

As an ESFP, one of your life goals is to experience as much as possible. In order to accomplish this, you are more than willing to step outside of your comfort zone. You will be sure to take others along with you on this journey and will have no issues with being the first to try anything. This also plays a part in social situations, as you are known for speaking your mind regardless of the situation. Of course you will try to do it in a tactful way, but there are times that this does not occur. When it happens, you can come across as more rude than bold to more sensitive listeners. Still, this characteristic also gives you quite the advantage when it comes to leadership positions.[21]

2. Your Originality Has No Bounds

Your type notices and loves to experiment with new styles. This often means that you will be the first among your friends to wear the newest trends or hear the latest song. It is very important to you that you stick out in the crowd instead of blending in. You will tend to avoid anything traditional and do not care about what others expect of you. When you are in a relationship, you also attempt to convince your partner of the wonders of bucking against mainstream expectations. If they prefer to follow the crowd, it is of no consequence to you, as you will quickly resume your in-depth exploration of everything you come across.

3. Ability to Appreciate and Create Beauty in Life

All ESFPs have a wonderful aesthetic sense that

allows them to decorate their home beautifully. You will throw in some classic art pieces here and there, but the majority of the house will feature bright and bold colors. You are not likely to follow any particular decorating rules, instead preferring to follow your instincts. Your fashion sense is much the same. You present an attractive and sophisticated image with tasteful and possibly expensive clothing. Overall, you have an appreciation for the finer things in life.[22]

4. Practicality Rules Your Life

The strong desire you have to experience life often means that your sense of practicality is strong. You prefer to see and do instead of dreaming and do not enjoy philosophizing. New or potential ideas need to be proven useful by science and experimentation before you trust them. For you, if something can be experienced with your five senses, that is even better. These traits combine to form an objective person who is able to use facts to make decisions when the situation warrants. You combine this sensibility with your Feeling (F) trait to make prudent and responsible determinations that benefit society.

5. You See What Others Do Not

Focusing on the present has its perks, particularly in your case. You have a knack for noticing how things work, even if you only try them once. Your Feeling (F) trait also provides you with an ability to accurately read others. In some careers, this talent may be used to defuse tensions between other employees or even patients. It also means that you are likely to be the one who spots trouble before it even occurs. Along with your ability to quickly adapt, this makes you an essential member of any organization.

6. The Best People Skills

As the "Performer" of the Myers-Briggs types, you have got to have excellent communication skills if you are going to get your point across. Your type is open-minded and genuinely loves people. You are talkative, witty, and never run out of things to discuss. Entertaining also comes naturally to you and you always seem to know the latest jokes and gossip. These skills come in handy when you are making new friends, an event that seems to occur wherever you go. All of these talents combine to draw people of all backgrounds to you.

7. Excitement and Enthusiasm for Life

This personality characteristic is perhaps one of your best. You want to experience as much as possible over your lifespan, whether it is has to do with love, career, food, or family. Your Sensing (S) trait means that you are extremely observant when it comes to the information that you draw in from the environment. This skill sometimes leads to overindulgence, as everything is perceived as wonderful. However, possibly the best aspect of this trait is that you go out of your way to make experiences as thrilling for others as they are for you.[23]

The 5 Greatest Areas of Improvement for an ESFP

For every strength trait you possess, there is also a weakness. As an ESFP, you may find yourself facing negative consequences quite regularly when your impulsiveness catches up to you. It is definitely the case that many of the following shortcomings are a natural consequence of your type's tendency to keep your life upbeat and exciting at all costs. Ironically, reining in these tendencies can lead to a more robust and fulfilling life.

1. You Can Be Too Sensitive

The ESFP is very emotional, which makes them especially vulnerable to criticism. You may feel attacked at the slightest provocation and blow things out of proportion. If you are not made aware of the appreciation others have for your efforts, you may become upset as well. When either of these situations occurs, you can become defensive or overly critical of others in an attempt to retaliate. This is the worst possible scenario though, and you are much more likely to use your charm to nip any tension in the bud. Your keen memory means that you have no problem remembering who said what, although it is not common for you to hold a grudge. According to 16personalities.com, "this is probably your greatest weakness, as it makes it hard to address any other weaknesses brought to light."

2. Acknowledging and Dealing with Conflict is Difficult

You tend to ignore and/or avoid conflict for as long as possible. Your usual method when it comes to this tendency involves saying or doing whatever is needed to resolve or lessen the issue. Immediately after, you will move on to searching for light-hearted and stimulating activities again. This can cause issues in many arenas of your life, particularly your career and romantic relationships. Conflict is inevitable in these two areas and an employee or leader who runs at the first sign of a disagreement will have difficulty going far. When it comes to romance, your mate may feel frustrated by your tendency to ignore important issues, and may feel as though they are not heard.

3. View Life in Two Ways: Exciting or Boring

On one hand, you are almost always involved in something exciting. On the other hand, if you are not being constantly stimulated, you may search for ways to create such occurrences for yourself and those around you. When this happens, more often than not, you can be found acting before thinking, engaging in risky behavior, or indulging yourself to the point of harm. Combined with your potential for distraction, you may jump from activity to activity with no regard for what is happening in the world around you. Others may become upset with your seemingly selfish tendency to forget your promises and duties.

4. The Future is of No Consequence to You

It is no secret that ESFPs rarely put emphasis on events of the past or future. Living day-to-day is more your style and you feel that every event is a learning experience. Besides, even if you do make a plan, things could change at any moment, rendering it useless, right? This attitude has led many an ESFP to make risky financial decisions that affect their relationships with their loved ones. The risk is compounded by your desire to be surrounded by pretty things. You may also find yourself relying on your partner to keep track of other important issues that could derail the relationship in the future. The lack of planning present in your life can also lead to a general feeling of being unprepared or overwhelmed at first when it comes to challenges thrown your way. With your inability to adequately handle stress, this can have disastrous consequences.

5. You Possess a Short Attention Span

Any task that can be categorized as tedious and detailed is likely to be a challenge for ESFPs and you may find yourself quickly becoming frustrated. If they are around, you may turn to your friends for help, but will grudgingly finish the task when they are not. It is difficult to sit still for long periods of time as you feel the need to be physically active. This means that even if you are being mentally stimulated with information that you find interesting, you may find that you are still easily distracted. In general, you may find that you have a preference for the beginning of a project, as it can be difficult to actually complete them. These situations are also complicated by your dislike of planning for the future.

What Makes an ESFP Happy?

Throughout your life, you are happiest when surrounded by people. Although you enjoy being in the spotlight as much as possible, you are also content to simply sit and converse with friends and family. Your home is likely to be a party spot, where you can be the perfect host who spends their time mingling and joking with others. This need for social contact does not lessen as you age and can be the deciding factor when it comes to your contentment.

With children, their personality type changes identities daily. You may decide to be a firefighter one day and a teacher the next. You are much like your adult counterpart, in that you are happiest when you are physically active. Parents of ESFP children will not have to entertain them, but they may be concerned about your choice of activity. Unfortunately, others may label you "hyperactive," which will thankfully have no effect on your self-image. Following your own path is much more important to you than fitting into the box. You enjoy classes that do not require you to memorize details and have minimal structure. You may be found in performing or fine arts classes especially and will spend your free time goofing around with your friends.[24]

In your career, you excel at working with any type of equipment. You might drive a bulldozer, chisel a sculpture, or fly a plane.[25] Any position where you can work on a team is ideal. You have the skills to motivate your co-workers and the ability to make a boring task fun.

It is also very important to ESFPs that they have a collection of techniques that they can choose from. To this end, you will spend hours upon hours perfecting your craft, particularly when it comes to the artistic and athletic fields.

As an ESFP, you are happiest when you are busy and you may take on several duties at once. Chaos has no effect on you and you may even enjoy the chance to prove to others how adaptable you are. Your type wants to be considered artistic and bold, so you will act accordingly. You long for others to see your graceful side and take pride in your ability to improvise performances where this may occur. A desire to live on the edge results in your position as one of the personality types most likely to take risks. Those who enjoy bungee jumping and skydiving may fall into the ESFP category more often than others. Daring and dangerous stunts are not the only ways you will fulfill this need, however. Many surgeons, defense lawyers, and "Wall Street wheeler-dealers" are ESFPs as well.[26]

You have a childlike curiosity about the world and absorb plenty of information from your surroundings wherever you go, becoming a virtual encyclopedia of facts. You are somewhat hedonistic, due to the focus on what your five senses can bring to your attention. Instant gratification is the best possible outcome for you and you have the ability to withstand stimulation for much longer than other types. Others will forsake this pleasure if it interferes with their charitable goals, but you are willing to find ways to achieve both. You may satisfy your desires through athletics, good food, art, or any variety of exhilarating activities.

You love being in love, although you may have a bit of difficulty staying in relationships. Being swept off your feet with extravagant displays of affection is sure to appeal to ESFP women. ESFP men will be sure to provide a constant supply of gifts presented in increasingly flamboyant ways to their mates. Whatever the case, your type will make their feelings known. You may surprise both your friends and loved ones on a regular basis and get a kick out of being surprised yourself.[27]

The inner child present in ESFPs makes them exciting and involved parents. You will explore the world alongside your children, making as many discoveries as they do. Having a large number of children appeals to you and it can be said that you are uniquely qualified to handle the challenges that may come along with taking care of such a family.

You tend to be happiest when you are constantly stimulated, with plenty of opportunities for new experiences. Although you may have a tendency to overindulge at times, your upbeat and optimistic attitude allows you to categorize these situations as necessary experiences. Following your instincts is sure to fill many areas of your life with exciting and pleasurable events.

What are Some Common Careers of an ESFP?

ESFPs have many talents that include superb communication skills, a love for and ability to handle spontaneity, and a high-energy disposition. Your ideal career will allow you to use any combination of these skills in an environment where others surround you.

As an ESFP, you prefer to learn from hands-on experience instead of a book. When faced with a problem, your practicality comes in handy as you find solutions that are based on a combination of facts and common sense. Since you have such a great talent for this area, you are often found in jobs that take place in fast-paced environments. Health-related fields fit this profile well and your type enjoys a large presence as EMTs and emergency room nurses. In these jobs, you will also use your innate ability to quickly size up a situation and find a way to calm frightened loved ones.

You also have a knack for alleviating any remaining tension after the stabilization of a patient.[28]

These talents also lend themselves to the easy establishment of a rapport between you and your clients. This is essential in many helping fields, such as social work, and ESFPs can often be found in jobs where they can enhance the lives of others. You can also accomplish this task as a veterinarian, thanks to your love for animals.

It is also important to remember that your type will be happiest when working in careers where you can be directly involved in the action. A job in the educational field can be quite satisfying for you, especially as a preschool or elementary school teacher. ESFPs love kids and any opportunity where they can release their own inner child is a huge bonus for them. Working with younger ages also puts you in direct contact with environments that are less structured and require spontaneity, two aspects that are very enjoyable to you.[29]

You may also enjoy a career as an athletic coach. The high energy level and physical activity necessary for this job come very easily to your type, particularly since many ESFPs are athletic themselves. With your upbeat and encouraging personality, your players will feel that they can accomplish anything. In fact, your enthusiasm and sociability are the prominent tools to your success in many fields.

Any career where you can "work the room" so to speak is likely to be one that you enjoy as well. ESFPs are happiest when they are talking to a variety of people and you feel very comfortable in crowds. Many of you may find yourselves in jobs that include flight attendants, waiters, and receptionists.[30]

Surprisingly, ESFPs do not tend to enjoy business-related careers as much. Although you have no issues juggling the multiple projects often required of you,

you hate conflict, which makes you less than fond of workplace politics. Freedom is also important to you and you feel that you should be able to work when and as you please, using your own methods. Environments with lots of rules and restrictions do not appeal to you. Therefore, ESFPs often enjoy real estate, where you can be out of the office, work with a variety of personalities, and work according to your own schedule. Your persuasive skills also ensure that careers as a public relations specialist and fundraiser are enjoyable.[31]

As the ESFP is known as the "performer," it should not come as a shock that they can be particularly happy working in the entertainment field. A career as a comedian could be hugely successful, thanks to your great timing when it comes to jokes. Your type is also found among photographers, dancers, musicians, and film producers.[32]

The ESFPs abundance of talents gives them

opportunities for success in many fields. Your laid-back and open-minded personality indicates that you can work with almost anyone, a skill that ensures that you will fit in seamlessly with any group or environment.

Common Workplace Behaviors of an ESFP

After they have found a meaningful and satisfying career, ESFPs will display many of the same behaviors, regardless of the environment or field. For the most part, your personality type will get along marvelously with co-workers and higher-ups, but your love for change and preference to keep every situation upbeat, can irritate some.

Your optimistic and friendly personality often leads to numerous attempts to inject fun into all situations, regardless of the task that is assigned. You will get the work done; however, it needs to happen on your terms and preferably, on your own time. That is not to say that you are impractical. In fact, you are not the type to even pay attention to theories or potential outcomes and will instead focus on generating practical and tangible results. If you get your way, the outcome of such a task will benefit society overall.[33]

Since you are so sociable, you prefer talking face-to-face and may only use email or other methods of communication when absolutely necessary. This works well for you, particularly because of your ability to understand others and their motivations. You are quite comfortable working with a variety of personalities and your open-mindedness often makes for a harmonious environment when you are around. This is good, since you are very sensitive and will shy away from any type of conflict, preferring to keep things light and upbeat. This inclination towards harmony often means that you are also an adept negotiator. A side effect is that you may annoy others who feel that you do not take things seriously when needed.[34]

It has been noted by many that ESFPs have the hardest time dealing with conflict between themselves and others when compared to other Myers-Briggs types. Your primary way of dealing with any confrontation is to deny it exists until it is no longer possible. When asked to give feedback on others, the ESFP will be honest. However, when it is your turn to receive feedback (especially negative) you may become very defensive. Still, if you feel that the feedback is coming from a good place, you will eventually come around and will even take it to heart.[35] This defensiveness however, is likely to happen with any source of contention if you can no longer ignore an issue. If you are extremely stressed or fatigued, you may even become "quiet and withdrawn or openly criticize others." Those who are insensitive, intolerant, or cynical may also irritate you.[36]

To keep the peace, you are willing to take responsibility and clean up after others or smooth over any issues they may have caused. You will pay the greatest attention to the potential forging or destruction of relationships and then consider the task at hand. In these instances, your practicality and creativity is of great use. You will define the problem, look at what others are currently doing and have done in the past, and incorporate the two into your problem-solving process. The big picture will be weighed last, if it is considered at all.

Another talent of ESFPs that comes in handy at work is their ability to adapt to change. In the workplace, you will brainstorm, grasp new techniques, and put those techniques to use rather quickly and efficiently. Helping you along the way is your innate sense of what computers should do and how to make them do it. Challenges excite you, but others would do well to remember that it might take you a few tries to bring around any much-needed change. This is most likely due to you getting caught up in the moment and enjoying what you have accomplished thus far.[37]

For this reason it is best to give ESFPs short-term projects. This is often your first choice as well, given your preference for anything short and to the point in your life. You will also prefer being given the freedom to complete tasks using your own methods. If you finish before the deadline, it is considered to be the mark of a good job if you are granted the ability to spend the remaining time doing as you wish. Your freedom and independence are very important to you and when this is lacking, you have no qualms with leaving a position. Your loyalty is generally to projects and people, not organizations.[38]

The ESFP is likely to be a productive and essential member of any company, thanks to their sociability, practicality, and ability to adapt to change. These qualities allow you to work effectively as a manager or subordinate, as long as your desire for freedom is respected.

ESFPs and Personal Relationships

ESFPs are popular people for many reasons. You are bubbly and wonderful conversationalists who are often generous with your time. Your desire to have fun wherever you go also draws many to you. You love to share every experience you have with your friends and loved ones. Excitement is contagious and you make it your mission to make everyone feel as caught up in the moment as you do. For ESFPs, your main priority in life is to feel as alive as possible.[39]

Your idea of fun is going to outings or participating in activities that engage all five senses. You should watch out for a tendency to take things too far and engage in risky or careless behaviors that lead to unforeseen (or ignored, as is usually the case for you) negative consequences. In these instances, you may even involve others in your hasty decisions.[40]

When it comes to your friends, you are warm and

caring. You are always available to listen to any troubles and your advice is practical and varies. However, you are extremely sensitive and will be offended at the slightest negative remark. It will not be easy to tell this since you do not let on that you are hurt, in an attempt to keep things light and harmonious. Instead, you usually hope that the problem will simply solve itself.[41]

One of the few instances in which you may express your disappointment is when friends or other loved ones reject your favorite pastimes or activities you plan to engage in. You will make it clear that you do not have time to be lectured and may even end the friendship right then and there.

It is a good thing making new friends is easy for your type then, thanks to your charming personality. Where you may fail is in keeping the friendships you already have. With your focus on the here and now instead of the past, you may forget that others do not have the same sense of adventure that you do. A desire on their part for peace and quiet may lead to you becoming bored with them once their novelty has worn off.

As a result, ESFPs may come across as shallow people who only care about their own pleasure. This is far from the truth, as you care deeply about your friends and will put a lot of effort into coming up with group experiences you think everyone will enjoy. Although it may not appear so, you are very distressed by the occasional conflicts that can end your friendships.[42]

When it comes to your romantic relationships, you are most likely to be attracted to those who share the same attitudes. Your personality type is happiest with lots of adventure in your life and this should have a part in all of your relationships. At its worst, this may mean that you may have trouble settling down with one partner. If this occurs, you may feel as though you cannot live your life to the fullest.[43]

You have no issues with reevaluating the relationship if your feelings change, which can be a potentially common occurrence. It is more likely that only mature and experienced ESFPs will understand that relationships that are enduring and possibly the most satisfying will take time and a conscious effort.[44]

ESFPs have almost the same attitude to parenting as they do to spending time with their friends. You make relaxed and fun-loving parents who genuinely love playing with your children. When they are young, you are constantly coming up with new ways to make every day as exciting as you can.

You will be sure to provide plenty of emotional support. Not surprisingly, your type is not known for being especially demanding parents, although you will administer discipline when necessary.[45]

At home, your well-developed aesthetic sense often means that you will live in a beautifully decorated space. You may spend a lot of money on the task of acquiring decorations or other items, sometimes at the expense of paying bills or helping your family out financially in other ways. If this occurs often, it may become a source of contention with your family.[46]

The sociable and charming ESFPs make it their goal to be surrounded by friends as often as possible. Your friendships can be brief or long lasting, but they are sure to provide fun times for everyone involved. Both romantic and parental relationships are much the same, with plenty of adventure and support given. In general, your personal relationships will be a source of happiness in your life.

ESFP: Parenting Style and Values

ESFPs have a good chance of taking the top spot among the Myers-Briggs types for being the most relaxed parents when it comes to raising their kids. Your type is also sensitive to their vulnerability, making you wonderful providers and protectors. Playing with your children speaks to the inner kid in you and you can always be counted on for coming up with creative games and activities.

As parents, you will love exploring the world alongside your children and sharing in their joy and wonder. When they ask questions you do not know the answer to, you will be the first to exclaim, "Let's find out!"[47] As ESFPs, you are known to encourage your child's exploration of their environment. Even better is the fact that you will allow them to do so in their own way. Since you tend to eschew schedules and take things as they come, your children will have many opportunities to make these discoveries on their own time as well.

Still, there are some rules in your household. ESFPs have a strong desire to keep their children from making the same mistakes and experiencing the same setbacks that they did when they were younger.[48] You are also adamant that they be respectful and follow the few rules that you do set. This attitude can lead to a brief period of time during the teenage years when you and your children clash. When this happens, you may suddenly switch from their friend to a stern authoritative parent. As with many other tendencies, you may take things too far, frustrating and confusing your children, particularly if they have strong Judging (J) traits. These Judging (J) types will expect stability and order and may become upset if they do not know what to expect from their ESFP parent.[49]

More likely is that you will count on your mate for any disciplining or providing of structure. Nevertheless, since you strongly believe that too much structure is not good for anyone, you may single-handedly undermine their influence when they attempt to create such an environment. This will not be done maliciously but if this occurs repeatedly, it could cause issues in your romantic and parental relationships. One lesson that ESFPs need to learn is that a little bit of structure can greatly benefit children as they grow up.[50]

Even though you are not fond of planning, no one would categorize you as impractical. You easily and adequately take care of your children's daily needs, no matter how big your family is. Your love for spontaneity and excitement in other areas of your life means that you will take on many of the responsibilities as the head of your family without being asked. Whether you can complete all of these tasks is another story and you may find yourself feeling a moment of guilt as you reflect on the things that did not get done at the end of the day.

Your family is very important to you and you seek to

provide them with the same joy and appreciation for life that you experience every day. At times, you may act somewhat impulsively, but it is difficult to stay angry with you, since you are always thinking of others. You can be sure that your children will affectionately remember you as "fun-loving, upbeat, and affectionate, if somewhat scattered."[51]

Why Do ESFPs Make Good Friends?

ESFPs are seldom found alone and often have a large circle of friends. Social gatherings give you lots of energy instead of taking it away, as is the case with Introverts (I).[52] You often like to involve your romantic partners in your social life as well. In most instances, you will put on a show for everyone, including your friends. There is always lots of laughter and soaking up attention on your part when you are with your friends and many would describe every outing as being reminiscent of a celebration.[53]

You prefer for things to remain light and happy between you and your friends, although your affection for them runs deep. You have the ability to genuinely enjoy life as you experience it and you want others to enjoy it as much as you do. To this end, you try to think of activities that everyone is sure to enjoy. Since you are very much in tune with your five senses, these outings will often revolve around food, alcohol, or music. You may go overboard when pursuing these interests and need to be careful that you do not drag others down with you.[54]

Friends who seek you out will find someone willing to listen to them vent about any and all problems, as well as give practical advice. You often have the ability to lift your friends' spirits with your good humor. Out of all of the Myers-Briggs types, you are considered the most generous and only the ISFP is known to be kinder. You will give freely without expecting anything in return. On the other hand, you will not hesitate to ask for help from your friends when faced with detailed or repetitive tasks.[55]

ESFPs get along with all types of people; although they usually are not willing to spend time with those they find boring. Those who expect you to relate to them intuitively or talk at length about theories and possibilities may not have a place in your social circle either. You are most likely to enjoy friends who are fellow Extroverts (E) and have the Feeling (F) trait.[56]

Your type has no difficulty making friends, although some may be put off by your blunt and straightforward personality. You may have difficulty keeping any friendships together for more than a short amount of time. In particular, you tend to be very sensitive and will take it personally if others do not agree with your fun-seeking and impulsive lifestyle. Your focus on the newness and originality present in budding relationships can also lead to a lack of nurturing that is needed to make them last. If you lose interest in a friendship, it is not uncommon for you to move on, regardless of how long it has lasted.

This tendency can sometimes lead others to assume that you do not truly care about anyone besides yourself. The truth is that your friendships are very important to you and may even be the source that comprises a large part of your happiness. As you mature, you may begin to respect and become more open to other personality types and approaches.[57]

ESFPs often seek the company of others in an attempt to surround themselves with friends. They accept the presence of many, although they prefer the company of other Extroverts (E). Whatever the case, your charismatic personality draws others to you naturally.

ESFP Romance

With your charisma and generous personality, it is not surprising that romantic relationships with your type are unforgettable. You love the feeling of being in love and will work hard to make your partners happy.

While ESFP women may have flirting down to a science, there is almost nothing they enjoy more than being wooed by a potential suitor. Grand gestures and of course, spontaneity are among the tactics that will catch your eye. Once you are in a relationship, you are very affectionate and love attending to your partner's physical needs.[58]

As an ESFP man, you make your significant other feel special with lots of compliments and thoughtful actions. You will spare no expense with gifts and will think of extravagant ways to present them. When bestowed along with the romantic games you like to engage in, it will not be hard for your partner to feel appreciated and adored.[59]

You love your relationships the most when they are in their infancy and feel fresh and new. This attitude fosters a tendency to avoid long-term commitment. If your significant other can recognize this trait and give you lots of space in the relationship, it may very well be the one of the keys to ending the cycle. Until then, you will focus mostly on enjoying the time that you spend with your significant other as much as possible.[60]

Your social tendencies mean that you often respect the input of others (particularly that of your friends) when it comes to your relationships. At times, you may give these opinions more power than they deserve and allow them to color important decisions that would best be contemplated on your own.

Any disagreement or conflict between you and your partner tends to make you very uncomfortable, as you may take anything said as a personal attack on your character. Your preferred way of dealing with these types of situations is to pretend that everything is fine, rather than discuss the issues. This can backfire, since your mate's dissatisfactions may not be expressed or explored until it is too late. If forced to, you may use your practical outlook to resolve the issues and then quickly move on to something more enjoyable.[61]

As an ESFP, you will prefer to let your actions express how you feel and will show your love through gifts and thoughtful and kind deeds. You will happily spend your time completing the practical tasks that help your household run smoothly, such as cooking or driving the kids to and from soccer practice. There may be a tendency to take on more than you can handle, particularly since you are easily distracted. It takes several attempts for you to finish projects or tasks given to you by your partner, so patience on their part is essential. At the end of the day, you love being told how much your actions have been appreciated, whether it is through words or gifts.

ESFPs love to keep their relationships exciting and may spend a lot of time coming up with ways to surprise their partners. You can be materialistic at times, so it is not unusual for these surprises to come with an expensive price tag. Your propensity for spending money can have some very positive effects when combined with your aesthetic sense, however. You are likely to be an attractive partner who takes care of themselves physically and is always dressed tastefully. The home you share with your significant other is likely to be beautifully decorated as well.[62]

If your feelings for your partner begin to change, you will immediately begin to re-evaluate the relationship. In fact, you may do this regularly, without any provocation. If you decide your feelings have changed for the worse, you will seriously consider breaking things off, regardless of the love you may have for them.

The best partners for you are those who can provide stability in your life. This usually includes people with the Judging (J) and Sensing (S) traits. Surprisingly, many have also found that your type fosters successful relationships with Introverts (I), although this may depend on the strength of your Extroversion (E) trait. ISFJs and ISTJs are among the best partners for you.[63]

ESFPs have no problem being affectionate and showing their appreciation for their partner by being helpful and giving them thoughtful gifts. You may only be committed on a day-to-day basis, but you will spend that time tending to your partner's happiness. Romantic relationships with your type are always full of adventure and new experiences.

7 Actionable Steps for Overcoming Your Weaknesses as an ESFP

When you are made aware of your strengths and weaknesses, you may begin to wonder if there are ways to develop and strengthen your natural talents. Here are 7 steps you can take to enhance the outcome of such a process:

1. Live in the Future

You have a tendency to rely on others to keep an eye on what lies ahead for you while you happily concern yourself with present matters. Keep in mind however, that there may not always be someone who is willing to, or who can, properly fulfill this task. Start slowly and take a moment to consider things like your retirement and ways you can supplement your income now. Or contemplate what your health might be like if you continue to indulge your preference for rich foods throughout your life without a thought of their toll on your body. The end goal is to realize and begin to plan for the inevitabilities of life.

2. Develop Your Judging (J) Trait

As a Sensing (S) and Perceiving (P) type, you usually prefer to deal with what can be seen or handled and like to keep your options open. This can lead to an indecisive and somewhat shallow personality, unless you spend time developing your Judging (J) trait. You can do this by occasionally scheduling things in advance instead of simply letting things happen. Another tactic is to make a decision and stick with it, regardless of how many new possibilities come up. Developing one of your less dominant characteristics is a lifelong chore, so remember that successes and setbacks are to be expected.[64]

3. Try to Not Take Things Personally

What may seem like a personal attack is sometimes just the opposite. Consider that a person who is questioning your methods may be genuinely interested in your technique or that a criticism is made with the intent to help. You will encounter many personality types in your life, each with their own way of interacting with others. If the goal is to achieve personal growth, then it is essential that you listen to advice from other sources. Remember that as your open-mindedness and objectivity are assets in other areas of your life, they can be in this one as well.

4. Be Responsible for Your Actions

When you get distracted (which happens quite often), you may find yourself forgetting to follow through on promises made to others. It is also the case that you will blame others for your misfortunes in the event that things do not turn out the way you had hoped. When faced with such situations, do not deny their existence and risk making a small issue into a bigger one. Being accountable for your behavior is a task you may struggle with, but it is also a necessary one to complete.

5. Learn to Deal with Conflict Properly

When immersed in conflict at work or in a relationship, you have trouble expressing your more negative emotions. You will hold them in, making your anxiety levels rise steadily until you can do this no longer and explode. Clearly, this can lead to some regrettable situations and a future goal might be learning to pull someone aside and talk through any issues you have. There are many tactics that do not involve dealing directly with the person you have disagreed with as well. Take note of these and seek to incorporate them into your life whenever they are needed.

6. Emphasize the Completion of a Task

The projects you start often remain unfinished, sometimes with a momentary sense of regret on your part. This is somewhat acceptable when it comes to your personal hobbies, but it can become an issue in other areas, specifically when you are at work or if you are in a leadership position. You must overcome this tendency when necessary, perhaps by setting up a reward system or breaking a task into smaller steps. Keep in mind that the ability to finish what you start is a skill that many both struggle with and overcome.

7. Learn to Deal with Stress

Your low tolerance for anxiety often leads to you feeling as though the world around you is unfair and out to get you. This is quite contrary to your normal happy-go-lucky personality and can come to the forefront when you are forced to deal with situations requiring careful consideration. Try keeping your unique personality quirks and needs in mind when dealing with such an event. For example, take frequent breaks to do something active when you find yourself becoming distracted or tense. There are many anxiety-reducing techniques that can be tailored to your temperament and being aware of these can help tremendously.

The 10 Most Influential ESFPs We Can Learn From

1. Justin Bieber

Whether you love or hate him, you have to admit that this entertainer has risen through the ranks rather quickly. He displays the ESFPs' tendency to seek as much pleasure as possible, often without thinking of potential consequences. Despite his very public mistakes, Bieber continues to be true to himself, a trait that should be admired.

2. Howard Schultz

The chairman and CEO of Starbucks first joined Starbucks as the Director of Marketing and decided to start his own coffee shop shortly after. His former employers were so impressed with his efforts that they sold the company to him, allowing him to take on the Starbucks name and use his business acumen to expand it to the giant corporation we know today.

Following his own path was instrumental in his success and he is a great example of never giving up on your dream.

3. Cameron Diaz

Former model and current actress Cameron Diaz is widely known for her happy-go-lucky personality. She had no ambitions of becoming a movie star when she was younger, but decided to audition for her breakout role in the film *The Mask* because of a modeling agent's recommendation. She won the role despite having no acting experience and successfully transitioned to the Hollywood world, thanks to her adaptability and spontaneous nature. Her natural positivity and zest for life are apparent both on-screen and off-camera.

4. Quentin Tarantino

This American director, producer, and screenwriter is famous for his often violent and satirical films. Like many ESFPs, his talents lie in the artistic realm and he dropped out of school at 15 to attend an acting class full-time. His enthusiasm for film-making shines through in his interviews and has led to many commercially successful movies, several of which have become cult favorites. The excitement he displays for his chosen career proves the importance of finding a path suited to your personality and dreams.

5. Deepak Chopra

An advocate of alternative medicine, Deepak Chopra is an example of a mature ESFP who has developed his strengths. After meeting the head of the Indian Council for Ayurvedic Medicine, he was inspired to give up his unhealthy habits. He began to partake in meditation to help him achieve this healthier lifestyle and has since written numerous books and articles on alternative medicine, in addition to speaking at many events. His willingness and ability to change for the better, as well as his attempts to help others do the same, are characteristics that every personality type should take note of.

6. Sir Paul McCartney

McCartney is one of the most successful musical artists and composers of all times, a most impressive feat. He showed a talent for music, as many ESFPS do, when he was a child. A self-taught musician, McCartney's skill with instruments has been praised by many other performers. After forming the Beatles and playing with them for over 10 years, he embarked on a successful solo career following the break-up of the band. The refinement of his musical talents and abilities has given McCartney opportunities that many only dream of.

7. Steve Irwin

Also known as the Crocodile Hunter, Irwin was an Australian wildlife expert. The enthusiasm and zest for life he possessed captivated the world and he was instrumental in introducing the natural world to many. Irwin successfully used his ESFP talents and showed us the importance of living life to the fullest.

8. John F. Kennedy

John F. Kennedy was the 35th President of the United States. During his time in office, many described him as laid-back and tolerant except when it came to boredom. The reforms that he made created tangible improvements in the lives of many. His willingness to act when necessary, even against popular opinion, is a characteristic found in many ESFPs.

9. Richard Branson

Best known as one of the founders of the Virgin Group, Branson started his first business at sixteen. His poor performance in school led to his teacher remarking that he would either "end up in prison or become a millionaire."[65] He surpassed those expectations by becoming a billionaire after forming several businesses that currently include an airline, phone, and train companies. His willingness to take risks is a common ESFP trait that should be appreciated by all.

10. Tony Robbins

In his words, Robbins childhood was difficult and abusive and he overcame it through sheer determination. To accomplish this, he used his abilities to read the body language of others and his innate talent for understanding human nature to catapult himself to stardom and a successful career. Surprisingly, he has no specialized training in life coaching and has used his ESFP ability to learn through direct experience to pick up the majority of his trade. From him, we can learn the value of hands-on experience.[66]

Conclusion

You are one of the few types with the ability to fully enjoy life and thrive as you meet the challenges it brings head-on. You attempt to selflessly share and promote this joy and enthusiasm in everyone you meet, making you a positive presence in their lives.

When left to your own devices, your creativity and resourcefulness come shining through. Your Extroversion (E) and Feeling (F) traits give you a sociable, caring, and tactful personality, which assists you in many areas of your life. It has particularly positive effects when it comes to your personal relationships and career. You have a knack for calming others in crisis and this is mostly due to the aforementioned qualities. The Sensing (S) and Perceiving (P) characteristics that you possess are also among your best attributes. When used appropriately, you are able to both realistically assess and determine the potentialities of situations. You use the incoming information from your five senses to accomplish this task, making you much more in tune with your body than the average person. To offset these skills, you can enhance the Judging (J) side of your personality. When this is accomplished, you will be more efficient in the ventures that you undertake. You may also gain the ability to better relate to those who are less spontaneous than you, shattering the irresponsible and flighty image you may portray to some.

Your personal relationships are a great source of happiness in your life and your friends, family, and mate often feel the same way. The affection and appreciation you show your loved ones leave no doubt as to how you feel about them. You are a born entertainer and your extravagant performances and story-telling acumen make every moment spent with you a thrilling and enjoyable adventure. A focus on cultivating your relationships for longer periods of time can take them to depths that they have never reached before.

Many famous ESFPs have shown how their ability to observe and quickly duplicate results through hands-on experience can be an extremely useful skill when it comes to achieving success. You can overcome almost any obstacle in life, thanks to your optimistic attitude and willingness to go in a new direction when other paths have led you astray. The influential people mentioned in the previous section are only a small subset of the vast number of ESFPs who have used their innate talents to provide practical and tangible solutions to both individual and societal ills.

The level of energy and enthusiasm you possess is rare among all Myers-Briggs types. When these attributes are used properly, they can enhance the cultivation of your best talents. Specifically, increasing your ability to commit to and follow through on the projects you have started can be very beneficial to the process of personal development. As you mature, you will learn how to successfully balance those areas that are most important to you. At that point, you will truly be able to experience all that life has to offer.

Final Word/About the Author

I was born and raised in Norwalk, Connecticut. Growing up, I could often be found spending afternoons reading in the local public library about management techniques and leadership styles, along with overall outlooks towards life. It was from spending those afternoons reading about how others have led productive lives that I was inspired to start studying patterns of human behavior and self-improvement. Usually I write works around sports to learn more about influential athletes in the hopes that from my writing, you the reader can walk away inspired to put in an equal if not greater amount of hard work and perseverance to pursue your goals. However, I began writing about psychology topics such as the Myers Brigg Type Indicator so that I could help others better understand why they act and think the way they do and how to build on their strengths while also identifying their weaknesses. If you enjoyed

ESFP: Understanding & Relating with the Performer please leave a review! Also, you can read more of my works on *INFPs, ENFJs, ISFPs, ISFJs, ESFJs, ESTJs, How to be Witty, How to be Likeable, How to be Creative, Bargain Shopping, Productivity Hacks, Morning Meditation, Becoming a Father,* and *33 Life Lessons: Success Principles, Career Advice & Habits of Successful People* in the Kindle Store.

Like what you read?

If you love books on life, basketball, or productivity, check out my website at claytongeoffreys.com to join my exclusive list where I let you know about my latest books. Aside from being the first to hear about my latest releases, you can also download a free copy of *33 Life Lessons: Success Principles, Career Advice & Habits of Successful People.* See you there!

End Notes

[1] Briggs Myers, Isabel. & McCaulley, Mary H. "Chapter 1." *Manual: A Guide to the Development and Use of the Myers-Briggs Type Indicator®.* 5th ed. Palo Alto: Consulting Psychologists Press, 1989. 11. Print

[2] Briggs Myers, Isabel. & McCaulley, Mary H. "Chapter 1." *Manual: A Guide to the Development and Use of the Myers-Briggs Type Indicator®.* 5th ed. Palo Alto: Consulting Psychologists Press, 1989. 13. Print.

[3] Briggs Myers, Isabel. & McCaulley, Mary H. "Chapter 1." *Manual: A Guide to the Development and Use of the Myers-Briggs Type Indicator®.* 5th ed. Palo Alto: Consulting Psychologists Press, 1989. 12. Print.

[4] Briggs Myers, Isabel. & McCaulley, Mary H. "Chapter 1." *Manual: A Guide to the Development and Use of the Myers-Briggs Type Indicator®.* 5th ed. Palo Alto: Consulting Psychologists Press, 1989. 13. Print.

[5] Briggs Myers, Isabel. & McCaulley, Mary H. "Chapter 1." *Manual: A Guide to the Development and Use of the Myers-Briggs Type Indicator®.* 5th ed. Palo Alto: Consulting

Psychologists Press, 1989. 12. Print.

6 Briggs Myers, Isabel. & McCaulley, Mary H. "Chapter 1."
Manual: A Guide to the Development and Use of the Myers-Briggs Type Indicator®. 5th ed. Palo Alto: Consulting
Psychologists Press, 1989. 12. Print.

7 Briggs Myers, Isabel. & McCaulley, Mary H. "Chapter 1."
Manual: A Guide to the Development and Use of the Myers-Briggs Type Indicator®. 5th ed. Palo Alto: Consulting
Psychologists Press, 1989. 12-13. Print.

8 Briggs Myers, Isabel. & McCaulley, Mary H. "Chapter 1."
Manual: A Guide to the Development and Use of the Myers-Briggs Type Indicator®. 5th ed. Palo Alto: Consulting
Psychologists Press, 1989. 11. Print.

9 "What Can I Do With My Personality Type? ESFP Careers
and Majors." *Ball State University.* N.p., n.d. Web.

10 "ESFP." *Personality Playbook.* N.p., n.d., Web.

11 Keirsey, David. "The Performer [ESFP]." *Please Understand
Me II: Temperament, Character, Intelligence.* 1st ed. Del-Mar:
Prometheus Nemesis Book Company, 1998. 69. Print.

[12] Keirsey, David. 69. Print.

[13] Keirsey, David. 69. Print.

[14] Briggs Myers, Isabel and Myers, Peter B. "Extraverted Sensing Supported By Feeling." *Gifts Differing: Understanding Personality Type."* 1st ed. Palo Alto: Davies-Black Publishing, 1995. 102. Print.

[15] Keirsey, David. 69. Print.

[16] Briggs Myers, Isabel and Myers, Peter B. 99. Print.

[17] Keirsey, David. 69. Print.

[18] Krebs Hirsh, Sandra A. and Kummerow, Jean M. "ISFJ: Introverted Sensing with Feeling." *Introduction to Type in Organizations.* 3rd ed. Palo Alto: Consulting Psychologists Press, 1993. 16. Print.

[19] "ESFP Summary." *Medical Mastermind Community.* N.p., n.d. Web.

[20] "ESFP Career." *16 Personalities.* N.p., n.d. Web.

[21] "ESFP Strengths & Weaknesses." *16 Personalities.* N.p., n.d. Web.

[22] "ESFP Strengths & Weaknesses." *16 Personalities.* N.p., n.d. Web.

[23] "ESFP Strengths & Weaknesses." *16 Personalities.* N.p., n.d. Web.

[24] Keirsey, David. 70. Print.

[25] Keirsey, David. 45. Print.

[26] Keirsey, David. 52. Print.

[27] "Artisan™ Portrait of the Performer: ESFP." *Keirsey.* N.p., n.d. Web.

[28] "ESFP: Extraverted, Sensing, Feeling, Perceiving." *Advising at Louisiana State University Alexandria.* N.p., n.d., Web.

[29] "ESFP: Extraverted, Sensing, Feeling, Perceiving." *Advising at Louisiana State University Alexandria.* N.p., n.d., Web.

[30] "ESFP: Extraverted, Sensing, Feeling, Perceiving." *Advising at Louisiana State University Alexandria.* N.p., n.d., Web.

[31] "ESFP: Extraverted, Sensing, Feeling, Perceiving." *Advising at Louisiana State University Alexandria.* N.p., n.d., Web.

[32] "ESFP: Extraverted, Sensing, Feeling, Perceiving." *Advising*

at Louisiana State University Alexandria. N.p., n.d., Web.

[33] "ESFP Summary." *Medical Mastermind Community.* N.p., n.d. Web.

[34] "ESFP Summary." *Medical Mastermind Community.* N.p., n.d. Web.

[35] "ESFP Career." *16 Personalities.* N.p., n.d. Web.

[36] "ESFP Summary." *Medical Mastermind Community.* N.p., n.d. Web.

[37] "ESFP Career." *16 Personalities.* N.p., n.d. Web.

[38] "ESFP Summary." *Medical Mastermind Community.* N.p., n.d. Web.

[39] "ESFP." *Personality Playbook.* N.p., n.d., Web.

[40] "ESFP Romantic Relationships." *16 Personalities.* N.p., n.d. Web.

[41] "ESFP." *Personality Playbook.* N.p., n.d., Web.

[42] "ESFP Friendships." *16 Personalities.* N.p., n.d. Web.

[43] "ESFP." *Personality Playbook.* N.p., n.d., Web.

[44] "ESFP Romantic Relationships." *16 Personalities.* N.p., n.d. Web.

[45] "ESFP Family." *16 Personalities.* N.p., n.d. Web.

[46] "ESFP." *Personality Playbook.* N.p., n.d., Web.

[47] "ESFP Family." *16 Personalities.* N.p., n.d. Web.

[48] "ESFP Family." *16 Personalities.* N.p., n.d. Web.

[49] "ESFP Relationships." *Personality Page.* N.p., n.d. Web.

[50] "ESFP Relationships." *Personality Page.* N.p., n.d. Web.

[51] "ESFP Relationships." *Personality Page.* N.p., n.d. Web.

[52] "ESFP." *David Markley.* N.p., n.d. Web.

[53] "ESFP." *Personality Playbook.* N.p., n.d., Web.

[54] "ESFP Relationships." *Personality Page.* N.p., n.d. Web.

[55] Keirsey, David. 69. Print.

[56] "ESFP Friendships." *16 Personalities.* N.p., n.d. Web.

[57] "ESFP Romantic Relationships." *16 Personalities.* N.p., n.d. Web.

[58] "Artisan™ Portrait of the Performer: ESFP." *Keirsey.* N.p., n.d. Web.

[59] "Artisan™ Portrait of the Performer: ESFP." *Keirsey.* N.p., n.d. Web.

[60] "ESFP Romantic Relationships." *16 Personalities.* N.p., n.d. Web.

[61] "ESFP Relationships." *Personality Page.* N.p., n.d. Web.

[62] "ESFP." *Personality Playbook.* N.p., n.d., Web.

[63] "ESFP Relationships." *Personality Page.* N.p., n.d. Web.

[64] Briggs Myers, Isabel and Myers, Peter B. 101. Print.

[65] "Richard Branson." *Wikipedia.* N.p., n.d. Web.

[66] "Why Tony Robbins Can't Pass ICF or IAC Life Coach Certification." *School of Coaching Mastery.* N.p., n.d. Web.

68245172R00055

Made in the USA
Middletown, DE
15 September 2019